SINGER + PIANO/GUITAR

VOCAL
SHEET
MUSIC

BROADWAY CLASSICS

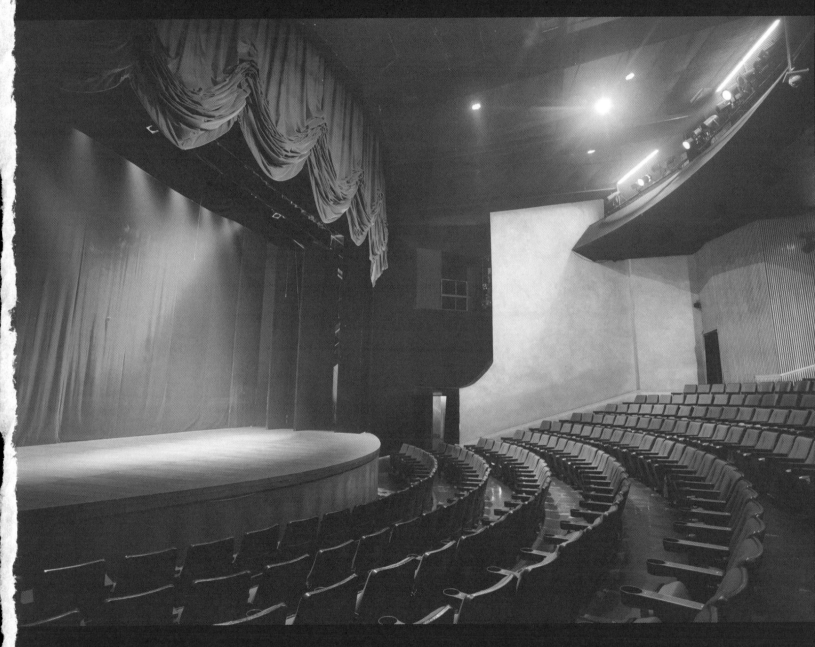

ISBN 978-1-5400-1536-5

HAL•LEONARD®

Visit Hal Leonard Online at
www.halleonard.com

Contact us:
Hal Leonard
7777 West Bluemound Road
Milwaukee, WI 53213
Email: info@halleonard.com

In Europe, contact:
Hal Leonard Europe Limited
42 Wigmore Street
Marylebone, London, W1U 2RN
Email: info@halleonardeurope.com

In Australia, contact:
Hal Leonard Australia Pty. Ltd.
4 Lentara Court
Cheltenham, Victoria, 3192 Australia
Email: info@halleonard.com.au

4 **Always True to You in My Fashion**
KISS ME, KATE

9 **Anyone Can Whistle**
ANYONE CAN WHISTLE

12 **As Long as He Needs Me**
OLIVER!

26 **Bewitched**
PAL JOEY

30 **But Not for Me**
GIRL CRAZY

17 **Cabaret**
CABARET

34 **Can't Help Lovin' Dat Man**
SHOW BOAT

38 **A Cockeyed Optimist**
SOUTH PACIFIC

42 **Diamonds Are a Girl's Best Friend**
GENTLEMEN PREFER BLONDES

46 **Don't Cry for Me Argentina**
EVITA

53 **Far from the Home I Love**
FIDDLER ON THE ROOF

56 **Goodnight, My Someone**
THE MUSIC MAN

60 **Hello, Young Lovers**
THE KING AND I

65 **I Could Have Danced All Night**
MY FAIR LADY

72 **I Dreamed a Dream**
LES MISÉRABLES

78 **I Enjoy Being a Girl**
FLOWER DRUM SONG

88 **I Got Rhythm**
GIRL CRAZY

92 **I Got the Sun in the Morning**
ANNIE GET YOUR GUN

100 **If I Loved You**
CAROUSEL

97 **If I Were a Bell**
GUYS AND DOLLS

106 **Make Someone Happy**
DO RE MI

113 **The Man I Love**
LADY BE GOOD

118 **Maybe This Time**
CABARET

123 **Memory**
CATS

130 **My Favorite Things**
THE SOUND OF MUSIC

139 **My Funny Valentine**
BABES IN ARMS

144 **On My Own**
LES MISÉRABLES

150 **Send In the Clowns**
A LITTLE NIGHT MUSIC

154 **The Simple Joys of Maidenhood**
CAMELOT

164 **Someone to Watch Over Me**
OH, KAY!

161 **Somewhere**
WEST SIDE STORY

168 **Tell Me on a Sunday**
SONG & DANCE

176 **Till There Was You**
THE MUSIC MAN

180 **Unexpected Song**
SONG & DANCE

184 **What I Did for Love**
A CHORUS LINE

190 **A Wonderful Guy**
SOUTH PACIFIC

173 **You'll Never Walk Alone**
CAROUSEL

ALWAYS TRUE TO YOU
IN MY FASHION

from KISS ME, KATE

Words and Music by
COLE PORTER

ANYONE CAN WHISTLE

from ANYONE CAN WHISTLE

Words and Music by
STEPHEN SONDHEIM

AS LONG AS HE NEEDS ME

from the Broadway Musical OLIVER!

Words and Music by
LIONEL BART

As long as he needs me ___ Oh yes he

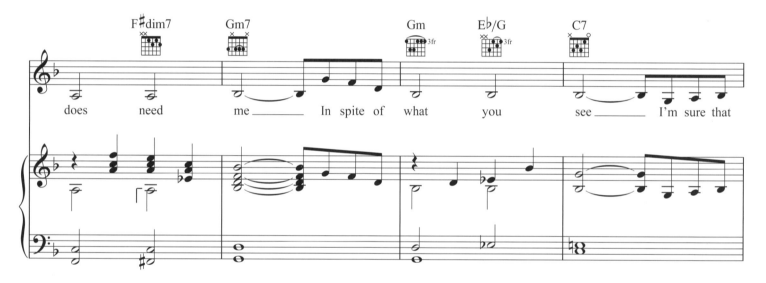

does need me ___ In spite of what you see ___ I'm sure that

he needs me ___ Who else would love him still ___ When they've been

CABARET
from the Musical CABARET

Words by FRED EBB
Music by JOHN KANDER

What good is sit-ting a-lone in your room?___ Come hear the mu-sic play.

Life is a cab-a-ret, old chum,___

BEWITCHED
from PAL JOEY

Words by LORENZ HART
Music by RICHARD RODGERS

Moderately, in 2

Freely, moving ahead

After one whole quart of brand-y Like a dai-sy I a-wake, With no Bro-mo-

Selt-zer hand-y I don't e-ven shake. Men are not a new sen-sa-tion;

I've done pret-ty well, I think. But this half-pint im-i-ta-tion Put me on the

This is the original show lyric. Hart fashioned a standard lyric that appears most often in print, and can be found in other publications.

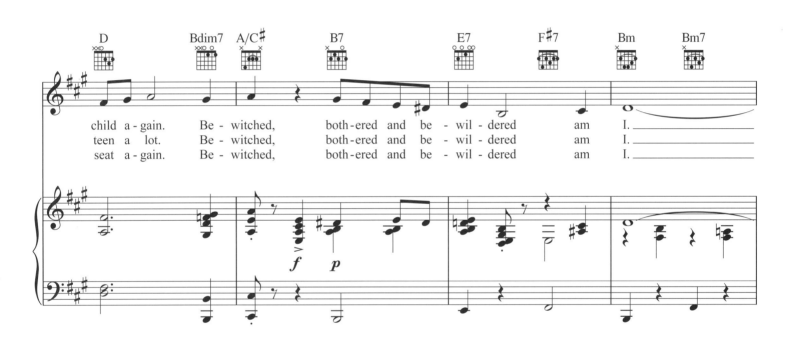

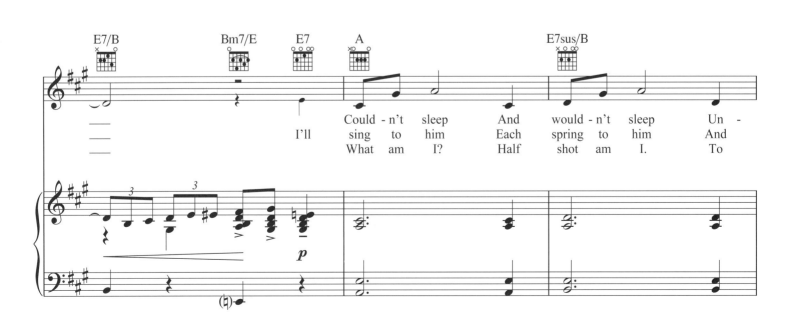

BUT NOT FOR ME
from GIRL CRAZY

Music and Lyrics by GEORGE GERSHWIN
and IRA GERSHWIN

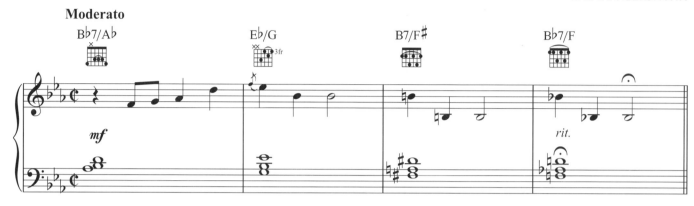

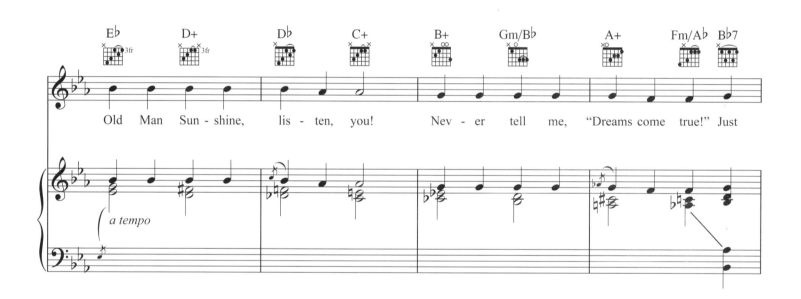

Old Man Sun-shine, lis-ten, you! Nev-er tell me, "Dreams come true!" Just

try it And I'll start a ri-ot. _____

Rather slow *(smoothly)*

CAN'T HELP LOVIN' DAT MAN

from SHOW BOAT

Lyrics by OSCAR HAMMERSTEIN II
Music by JEROME KERN

A COCKEYED OPTIMIST
from SOUTH PACIFIC

Lyrics by OSCAR HAMMERSTEIN II
Music by RICHARD RODGERS

DIAMONDS ARE A GIRL'S BEST FRIEND

from GENTLEMEN PREFER BLONDES

Words by LEO ROBIN
Music by JULE STYNE

DON'T CRY FOR ME ARGENTINA

from EVITA

Words by TIM RICE
Music by ANDREW LLOYD WEBBER

Tempo I

Tempo I

But all you have to do is look at me to know that ev-'ry word is true.

FAR FROM THE HOME I LOVE

from FIDDLER ON THE ROOF

Words by SHELDON HARNICK
Music by JERRY BOCK

GOODNIGHT, MY SOMEONE

from Meredith Willson's THE MUSIC MAN

By MEREDITH WILLSON

Moderato

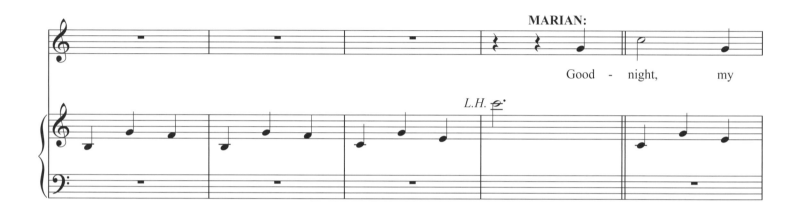

MARIAN:

Good - night, my

some - one, good - night, my love. Sleep tight, my some - one, sleep

Freely

C6 Dm7 G7 C6 C9sus C7 B♭/F F E♭9

tight, my love. Our star is shin - ing its bright - est

HELLO, YOUNG LOVERS
from THE KING AND I

Lyrics by OSCAR HAMMERSTEIN II
Music by RICHARD RODGERS

I COULD HAVE DANCED ALL NIGHT

from MY FAIR LADY

Words by ALAN JAY LERNER
Music by FREDERICK LOEWE

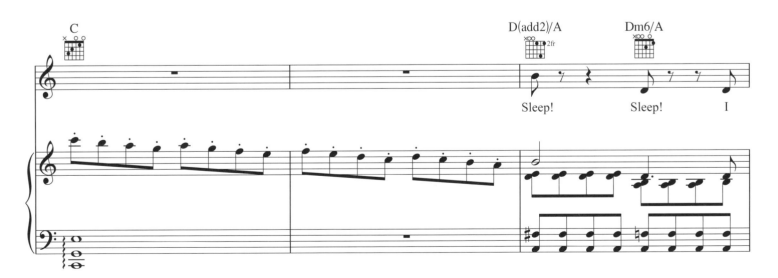

I DREAMED A DREAM
from LES MISÉRABLES

Music by CLAUDE-MICHEL SCHÖNBERG
Lyrics by ALAIN BOUBLIL, JEAN-MARC NATEL
and HERBERT KRETZMER

I ENJOY BEING A GIRL
from FLOWER DRUM SONG

Lyrics by OSCAR HAMMERSTEIN II
Music by RICHARD RODGERS

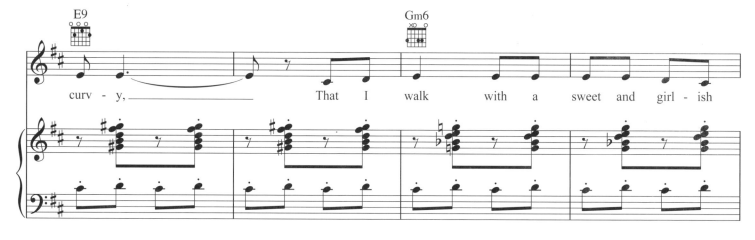

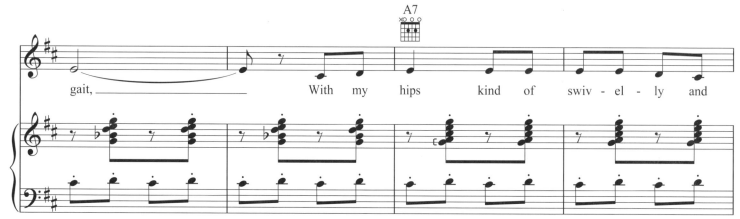

I GOT RHYTHM

from GIRL CRAZY

Music and Lyrics by GEORGE GERSHWIN
and IRA GERSHWIN

Days can be sun-ny, With nev-er a sigh; Don't need what mon-ey can buy. Birds in the tree sing Their day-ful of song, Why should-n't

G/D D7 G A♯dim D7/A G G6 Am7 D7
B♭/F F7 B♭ C♯dim F7/C B♭ B♭6 Cm7 F7
ask for an - y - thing more? I got dais - ies
G6/D C♯dim/D Am7 D7sus D7 G G6 Am7 D7 Cm6/D
4fr
B♭6/F Edim/F Cm7 F7sus F7 B♭ B♭6 Cm7 F7 E♭m6/F
In green pas - tures, I got my man. Who could
G/D D7sus D7 G B7 A/B Bdim B9
B♭/F F7sus F B♭ D7 C/D Ddim D9
ask for an - y - thing more? Old Man Trou - ble,
E B+ Bm/E E7/B A7 G/A Adim A9
G D+ Dm/G G7/D C7 B♭/C Cdim C9
I don't mind him, You won't find him

I GOT THE SUN IN THE MORNING

from the Stage Production ANNIE GET YOUR GUN

Words and Music by
IRVING BERLIN

IF I WERE A BELL
from GUYS AND DOLLS

By FRANK LOESSER

IF I LOVED YOU

from CAROUSEL

Lyrics by OSCAR HAMMERSTEIN II
Music by RICHARD RODGERS

Moderato espressivo

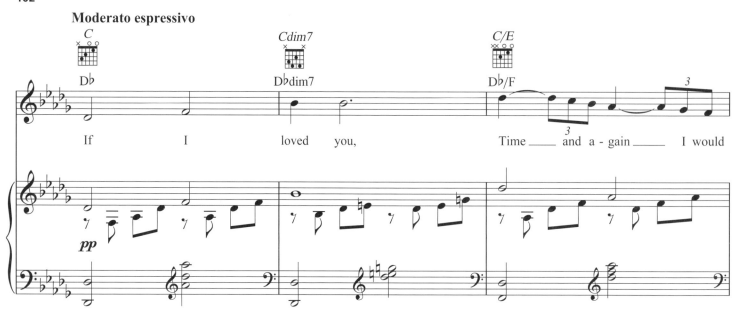

If I loved you, Time ____ and a - gain ____ I would

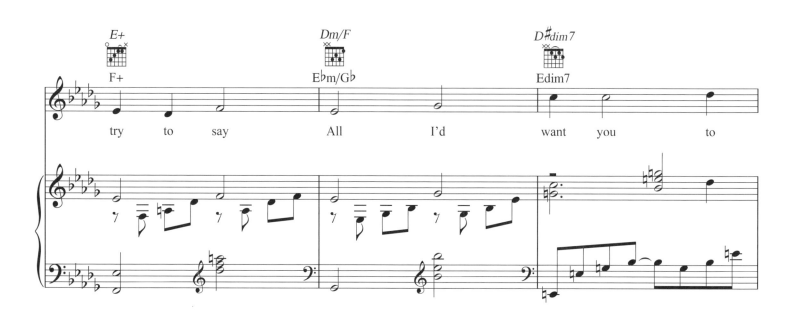

try to say All I'd want you to

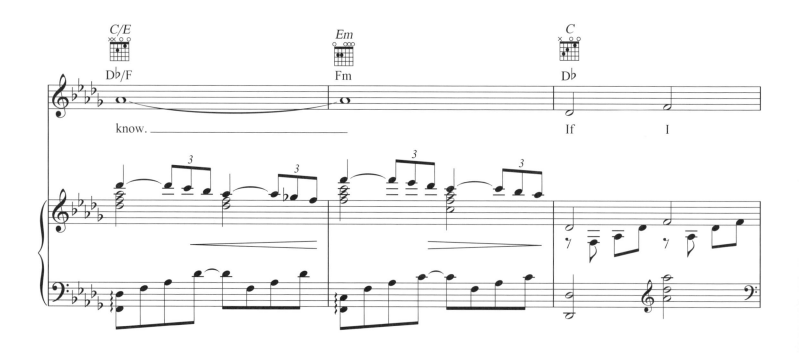

know. ____ If I

MAKE SOMEONE HAPPY
from DO RE MI

Words by BETTY COMDEN and ADOLPH GREEN
Music by JULE STYNE

THE MAN I LOVE

from LADY BE GOOD

Music and Lyrics by GEORGE GERSHWIN
and IRA GERSHWIN

Più mosso, con bravura

Andante

When the mel-low moon be-gins to beam, ev-'ry night I dream a lit-tle dream;

and, of course, Prince Charm-ing is the theme: the he for me. Al-

though I re-al-ize as well as you it is sel-dom that a dream comes true,

MAYBE THIS TIME
from the Musical CABARET

Words by FRED EBB
Music by JOHN KANDER

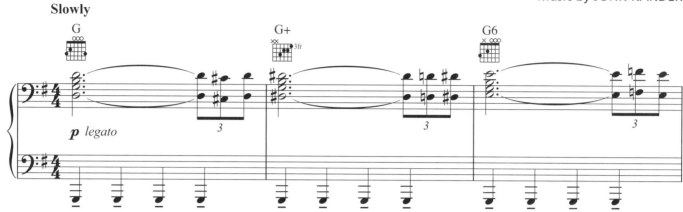

Steadily building

MEMORY

from CATS

Music by ANDREW LLOYD WEBBER
Text by TREVOR NUNN after T.S. ELIOT

Burnt out ends of smo - ky days; ___ the stale, cold smell ___ of

morn - ing. _____ The street lamp dies, an - oth - er
night is o - ver, ___ an - oth - er day is
dawn - ing.   Touch me. _____ It's so eas - y to
leave me _____ all a - lone with the mem - ory _____ of my days in the

MY FAVORITE THINGS
from THE SOUND OF MUSIC

Lyrics by OSCAR HAMMERSTEIN II
Music by RICHARD RODGERS

MY FUNNY VALENTINE

from BABES IN ARMS

Words by LORENZ HART
Music by RICHARD RODGERS

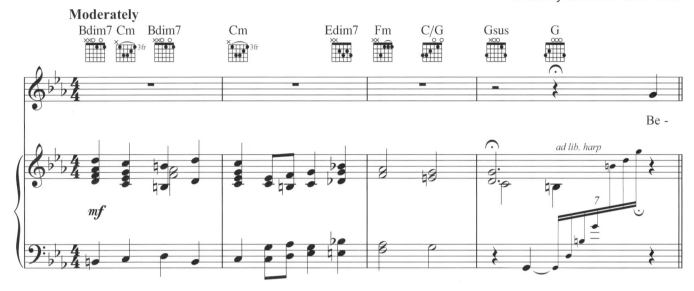

Moderately

Be -

Freely (*unaccompanied*)

N.C.

hold the way our fine feath-ered friend his vir - tue doth pa - rade. Thou

know - est not, my dim - wit - ted friend, the pic - ture thou hast made. Thy

va - cant brow and thy tous - led hair con - ceal thy good in - tent. Thou

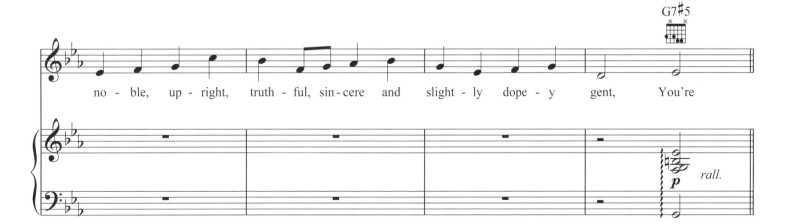

no - ble, up - right, truth - ful, sin - cere and slight - ly dop - e - y gent, You're

ON MY OWN

from LES MISÉRABLES

Music by CLAUDE-MICHEL SCHÖNBERG
Lyrics by ALAIN BOUBLIL, JEAN-MARC NATEL,
HERBERT KRETZMER, JOHN CAIRD and TREVOR NUNN

EPONINE:

And now I'm all a-lone a-gain, no-where to turn, no one to go to.

SEND IN THE CLOWNS

from the Musical A LITTLE NIGHT MUSIC

Words and Music by
STEPHEN SONDHEIM

THE SIMPLE JOYS OF MAIDENHOOD

from CAMELOT

Words by ALAN JAY LERNER
Music by FREDERICK LOEWE

SOMEWHERE
from WEST SIDE STORY

Lyrics by STEPHEN SONDHEIM
Music by LEONARD BERNSTEIN

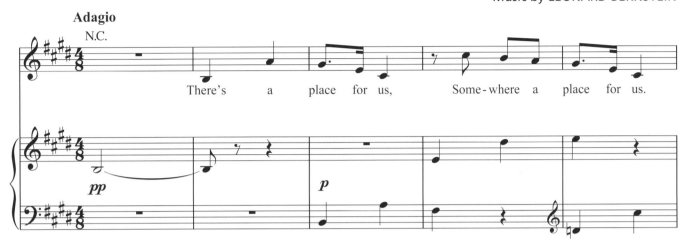

There's a place for us, Some-where a place for us.

Peace and qui-et and o-pen air Wait for us Some-where. __ There's a

time for us, Some-day a time for us, Time to-geth-er with

In the show the song is sung by a character simply known as "A Girl."

SOMEONE TO WATCH OVER ME

from OH, KAY!

Music and Lyrics by GEORGE GERSHWIN
and IRA GERSHWIN

TELL ME ON A SUNDAY

from SONG & DANCE

Music by ANDREW LLOYD WEBBER
Lyrics by DON BLACK

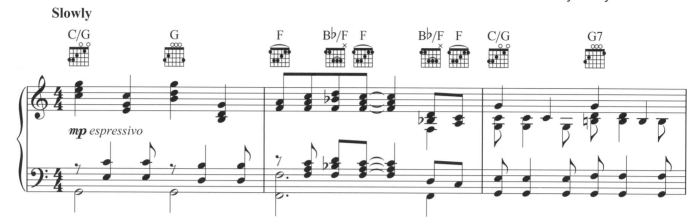

Don't write a let-ter when you want to leave,

don't call me at 3 a.m. from a friend's a-part-ment; I'd like to choose how I

YOU'LL NEVER WALK ALONE

from CAROUSEL

Lyrics by OSCAR HAMMERSTEIN II
Music by RICHARD RODGERS

TILL THERE WAS YOU
from Meredith Willson's THE MUSIC MAN

By MEREDITH WILLSON

UNEXPECTED SONG
from SONG & DANCE

Music by ANDREW LLOYD WEBBER
Lyrics by DON BLACK

I
I have nev-er felt like this, for once I'm lost for
I don't know what's go-ing on, can't work it out at

words your smile has real-ly thrown me.
all. What-ev-er made you choose me?

This is not like me at all, I nev-er thought I'd
I just can't be-lieve my eyes, you look at me as

WHAT I DID FOR LOVE

from A CHORUS LINE

Music by MARVIN HAMLISCH
Lyric by EDWARD KLEBAN

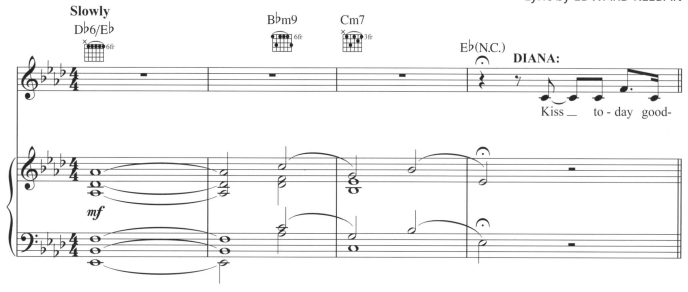

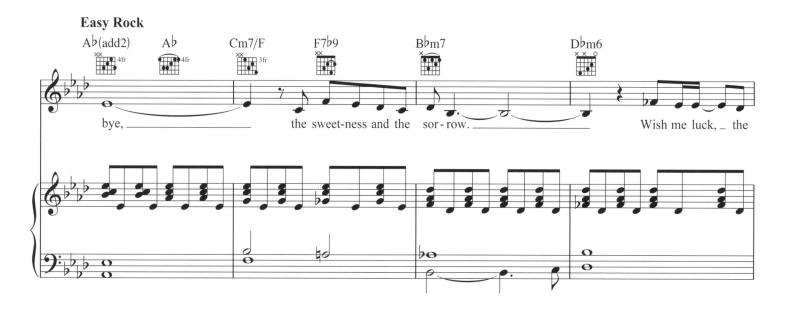

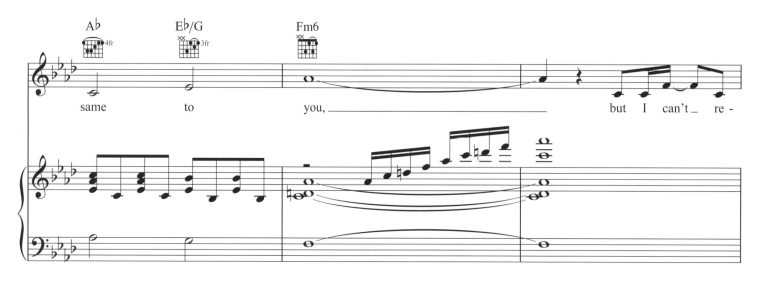

A WONDERFUL GUY

from SOUTH PACIFIC

Lyrics by OSCAR HAMMERSTEIN II
Music by RICHARD RODGERS

THE SINGER'S MUSICAL THEATRE ANTHOLOGY

The World's Most Trusted Source for Great Theatre Literature for Singing Actors

Compiled and Edited by Richard Walters

The songs in this series are vocal essentials from classic and contemporary shows – ideal for the auditioning, practicing or performing vocalist. Each of the eighteen books contains songs chosen because of their appropriateness to that particular voice type. All selections are in their authentic form, excerpted from the original vocal scores. Each volume features notes about the shows and songs. There is no duplication between volumes.

VOLUME 1

SOPRANO
(REVISED EDITION)
00000483 Book/Online Audio $42.99
00361071 Book Only.....................$22.99
00740227 2 Accompaniment CDs..$22.99

MEZZO-SOPRANO/BELTER
(REVISED EDITION)
00000484 Book/Online Audio $44.99
00361072 Book Only.....................$22.99
00740230 2 Accompaniment CDs..$22.99

TENOR
(REVISED EDITION)
00000485 Book/Online Audio $44.99
00361073 Book Only.....................$22.99
00740233 2 Accompaniment CDs..$24.99

BARITONE/BASS
(REVISED EDITION)
00000486 Book/Online Audio $44.99
00361074 Book Only.....................$24.99
00740236 2 Accompaniment CDs..$22.99

DUETS
00000487 Book/Online Audio $42.99
00361075 Book Only.....................$22.99
00740239 2 Accompaniment CDs..$22.99

VOLUME 2

SOPRANO
(REVISED EDITION)
00000488 Book/Online Audio $44.99
00747066 Book Only.....................$22.99
00740228 2 Accompaniment CDs..$24.99

MEZZO-SOPRANO/BELTER
(REVISED EDITION)
00000489 Book/Online Audio $44.99
00747031 Book Only.....................$22.99
00740231 2 Accompaniment CDs..$24.99

TENOR
00000490 Book/Online Audio $44.99
00747032 Book Only.....................$24.99
00740234 2 Accompaniment CDs..$24.99

BARITONE/BASS
00000491 Book/Online Audio $44.99
00747033 Book Only.....................$24.99
00740237 2 Accompaniment CDs..$22.99

DUETS
00000492 Book/Online Audio $44.99
00740331 Book Only.....................$24.99
00740240 2 Accompaniment CDs..$24.99

VOLUME 3

SOPRANO
00000493 Book/Online Audio $42.99
00740122 Book Only.....................$22.99
00740229 2 Accompaniment CDs..$24.99

MEZZO SOPRANO/BELTER
00000494 Book/Online Audio $44.99
00740123 Book Only.....................$22.99
00740232 2 Accompaniment CDs..$24.99

TENOR
00000495 Book/Online Audio $44.99
00740124 Book Only.....................$22.99
00740235 2 Accompaniment CDs..$22.99

BARITONE/BASS
00000496 Book/Online Audio $44.99
00740125 Book Only.....................$24.99
00740238 2 Accompaniment CDs..$24.99

VOLUME 4

SOPRANO
00000497 Book/Online Audio $42.99
00000393 Book Only.....................$22.99
00000397 2 Accompaniment CDs..$24.99

MEZZO SOPRANO/BELTER
00000498 Book/Online Audio $44.99
00000394 Book Only.....................$22.99
00000398 2 Accompaniment CDs..$22.99

TENOR
00000499 Book/Online Audio $44.99
00000395 Book Only.....................$22.99
00000399 2 Accompaniment CDs..$24.99

BARITONE/BASS
00000799 Book/Online Audio $44.99
00000396 Book Only.....................$24.99
00000401 2 Accompaniment CDs..$24.99

VOLUME 5

SOPRANO
00001162 Book/Online Audio $44.99
00001151 Book Only.....................$24.99
00001157 2 Accompaniment CDs..$22.99

MEZZO-SOPRANO/BELTER
00001163 Book/Online Audio $42.99
00001152 Book Only.....................$24.99
00001158 2 Accompaniment CDs..$24.99

TENOR
00001164 Book/Online Audio $44.99
00001153 Book Only.....................$24.99
00001159 2 Accompaniment CDs..$22.99

BARITONE/BASS
00001165 Book/Online Audio $44.99
00001154 Book Only.....................$24.99
00001160 2 Accompaniment CDs..$24.99

VOLUME 6

SOPRANO
00145264 Book/Online Audio $42.99
00145258 Book Only.....................$22.99
00151246 2 Accompaniment CDs..$22.99

MEZZO-SOPRANO/BELTER
00145265 Book/Online Audio $42.99
00145259 Book Only.....................$22.99
00151247 2 Accompaniment CDs..$22.99

TENOR
00145266 Book/Online Audio $42.99
00145260 Book Only.....................$22.99
00151248 2 Accompaniment CDs..$22.99

BARITONE/BASS
00145267 Book/Online Audio $42.99
00145261 Book Only.....................$24.99
00151249 2 Accompaniment CDs..$22.99

THE SINGER'S MUSICAL THEATRE ANTHOLOGY – "16-BAR" AUDITION

00230039 Soprano Edition............$24.99
00230040 Mezzo-Soprano Edition .$24.99

TEEN'S EDITION

SOPRANO
00230047 Book/Online Audio $39.99
00230043 Book Only.....................$22.99
00230051 2 Accompaniment CDs..$22.99

MEZZO-SOPRANO/ALTO/BELTER
00230048 Book/Online Audio $42.99
00230044 Book Only.....................$21.99
00230052 2 Accompaniment CDs..$22.99

TENOR
00230049 Book/Online Audio $39.99
00230045 Book Only.....................$22.99
00230053 2 Accompaniment CDs..$24.99

BARITONE/BASS
00230050 Book/Online Audio $39.99
00230046 Book Only.....................$19.99
00230054 2 Accompaniment CDs..$24.99

HAL•LEONARD®

Prices, contents, and availability are subject to change without notice.

Please visit **www.halleonard.com**
for complete contents listings.